MW01634920

List of abbreviations

cm – centimetre
tbsp – tablespoon
tsp – teaspoon
l – litre
ml – millilitre
pkt. – packet

5 4 3 2 1
ISBN 978-3-88117-774-0
Design: Niels Bonnemeier
Translation: Martina Birkhoff, Claire Agius
Editing: Monika Römer
© 2008 Verlag W. Hölker GmbH, Münster
www.hoelker-verlag.de

All right reserved.
Printed in Italy

Renate Wagner-Wittula
Christoph Wagner

The little Austrian Cookbook

Hölker Verlag

Contents

Unless otherwise stated, all recipes
are based on 4 servings.

Introduction

What makes Austrian cuisine really special is the fact that its most famous dishes do not actually originate from Austria! The Wiener Schnitzel, for example, is a slight variation on the Costoletta Milanese, the Strudel is in fact a Turkish creation, and Knödel (or dumplings) owe their culinary success to chefs in Bohemia. The famous Viennese Siedefleisch (boiled beef) – from the Tafelspitz through to the Schulterscherzl – bears a striking similarity to the Italian Bollito misto. The Viennese goulash comes from the Hungarian Gulyás, which – just to make things really complicated – is more of a goulash soup than an actual stew.

So what exactly is this Austrian cuisine, which is more commonly referred to as "Viennese cuisine" and is considered to be a multi-ethnical cuisine, having "stolen" the most delicious delicacies from the farthest corners of the old Austro-Hungarian Empire?

It is not only typical Viennese style of cooking that can be found in Austrian kitchens. There are many different culinary methods coming from the mountains, the valleys, the wine-growing and bread-basket regions, the farmsteads and the villages. Effectively, the keynotes in this culinary symphony are the following: Sterzen (Mashes), Nocken (Mini Dumplings), Knödel (Dumplings) and Schmarren (Shredded Pancakes). In their varied forms, they determine the layout of the Austrian table.

Meat dishes play a huge role in Austrian cuisine, particularly with regard to storage of provisions, salt-curing, smoking or preparation in the form of aspic. The prominence of roast pork on the menus in many rural hotels should not belie the fact that the culinary wealth of ideas of the country is, in reality, much more extensive. We only have to think of Kärntner Kasnudel (Carinthian Stuffed Cheesy Dough Pockets), Waldviertler Knödel (Potato Dumplings), Tiroler Leber (Tyrol Style Liver) or Salzburger Nockerl (Salzburg Egg Soufflé). In addition to these culinary delights, Austria can also boast a vast range of soups and soup ingredients, from the Frittatensuppe (Soup with Strips of Pancake) and Liver Dumpling Soup to Styrian Pumpkin Soup.

Although, Austria's Mehlspeiskuchl (desserts and sweet pastries) strongly reflect many influences from Bohemian cuisine, its numerous tortes, yeast-based and ring-shaped pastries, strudels, stollens, festive pastries and Mozartkugeln (chocolate-coated balls of marzipan with a nougat centre) have contributed to its reputation as a bona-fide "pastry paradise". This paradise is renowned not only in Vienna but throughout the surrounding areas, where the waltzes of Johann Strauß' (father and son) accompany these sweet temptations.

Soups & Starters

Soup with Strips of Pancake
Frittatensuppe

Serves 4–5

approx. 75 g plain flour,
125 ml milk, 2 eggs, salt,
oil for frying, 1 l hot beef stock,
chopped parsley to garnish

In a bowl beat the flour, milk, eggs and salt together to form a smooth crêpe-like batter. Heat a little oil in a small pan and fry 3–4 of the crêpes in succession (recipe p. 71). Roll up each crêpe and cut into fine strips using a sharp knife. Spread the strips out in warmed soup bowls, pour the hot beef stock over the strips and garnish with chopped parsley.

The pancakes can be further complemented by freshly chopped herbs.

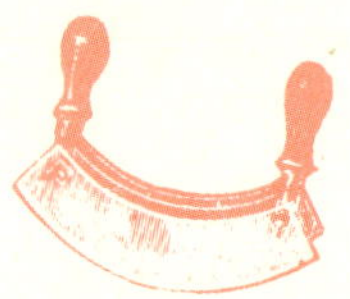

Herby Biscuit Soup
Kaiserschöberlsuppe

Serves 6

3 eggs, 3 tbsp butter (at room temp.),
2 tbsp milk, 4 tbsp plain flour, salt,
1 pinch of freshly ground nutmeg,
2 tbsp grated cheese,
butter and flour for batter and baking tray,
1 1/2 l hot beef stock,
chopped parsley or chives to garnish

Preheat the oven to 200 °C. Separate the eggs. Cream butter until fluffy and mix with milk, flour and the egg yolks to form a batter. Mix in the salt, nutmeg and grated cheese. Beat the egg whites with a pinch of salt until stiff and fold into the mix. Spread to a thickness of about 1 centimeters on a greased and flour-dusted baking tray. Bake in the oven for 15 minutes until golden. Leave to cool and cut into squares or rhombs. Slightly warm the Kaiserschöberl (biscuits) – preferably in the oven – immediately before serving. Then lay them in warmed soup bowls and pour the hot stock over. Garnish with parsley or chives.

Semolina Dumpling Soup
Grießnockerlsuppe

Serves 6

3–4 tbsp butter (at room temp.), 1 egg,
150 g semolina, salt, 1 pinch of freshly ground
nutmeg, 1 1/2 l hot beef stock,
chopped chives to garnish

Cream butter until fluffy and carefully mix in the egg and then the semolina. Season with salt and nutmeg. Leave the mixture to rest a while.

In the meantime boil ample salted water in a large pan. Dip 2 tablespoons in water and use them to make finger-shaped dumplings from the dough. Place them in simmering water for 5 minutes. Remove the pan from the heat and leave the dumplings for a further 10 minutes. Arrange the dumplings on warmed soup plates. Pour the hot beef stock over them and garnish with chives.

Liver Dumpling Soup
Leberknödelsuppe

Serves 6

200 g pork liver,
white bread (crust on),
a little milk for soaking,
1 spring onion, butter for sautéing,
1 tbsp chopped parsley,
1 egg, 100 g butter, 100 g breadcrumbs,
salt, freshly milled pepper,
1 pinch of marjoram,
1 1/2 l hot beef stock,
chopped parsley or chives to garnish

Place the liver on the chopping board and slice very thinly with a sharp knife. Soak the bread in the milk. Peel and finely chop the onion. Lightly brown the onion in the butter and mix in the chopped parsley. Squeeze the surplus milk from bread. Mix all this in thoroughly with the liver. Pass the mixture through a sieve, mix in the egg, butter and breadcrumbs. Season with salt, pepper and marjoram. Leave to rest for 1/2 hour.
With moistened hands, shape small dumplings from the dough and cook them in gently simmering salted water, until they rise to the surface. Remove the pan from the heat and leave the dumplings in the water for a further 5 minutes. Arrange the dumplings on warmed soup plates and pour the hot beef stock over them. Garnish with parsley or chives and serve.

Tyrol Style Dumpling Soup
Tiroler Knödelsuppe

Serves 6

approx. 200 g breadcrumbs,
50 g Tyrol bacon, 50 g cured sausage
(e.g. salami), 125 ml milk, 2 eggs, salt,
1 pinch of freshly ground nutmeg,
1 tbsp chopped parsley, 40 g plain flour,
1 1/2 l hot beef stock, chopped chives to garnish

Mix the breadcrumbs with diced bacon and the very finely chopped sausage in a bowl. Whisk the milk and eggs together in a separate bowl and season with salt, nutmeg and parsley. Pour the mixture over the breadcrumbs. Leave to soak for 15 minutes, then fold in the flour. Alter the dough to the desired consistency by adding milk or flour as necessary. With moistened hands, shape small dumplings from the dough. Leave the dumplings to cook in salted water for 10–15 minutes, until they rise to the surface. Place 2 dumplings on each warmed soup plate, pour the beef stock over them and garnish with chives.

Tiroler Knödel are often eaten as a main course, in which case they should be shaped into larger dumplings and served with sauerkraut or salad.

Styrian Pumpkin Soup
Steirische Kürbissuppe

Serves 4–6

600 g of yellow pumpkin flesh, 1 onion,
2 tbsp clarified butter, 1 tbsp plain flour,
1 substantial dash of Styrian Welschriesling for infusing (or a similar dry white wine), 3/4 l beef stock,
1/4 l whipped cream, salt, freshly milled pepper,
1 pinch of freshly ground nutmeg, 2 tbsp pumpkin seeds, small amount of fat (for roasting seeds)
Pumpkin seed oil to season

Scrape out the pumpkin flesh, removing any stringy fibres and seeds. Dice into small cubes. Peel onion and chop finely. Brown off in clarified butter and add the pumpkin cubes. Let sauté for a few minutes. Sprinkle the flour into the pan and stir in well. Pour in the white wine. Add beef stock and whipped cream, season with salt and pepper, mix well again. Cover the vegetables and leave them to stew for about 30 minutes, until soft.
Pass the pumpkin through a sieve or purée using an immersion blender. Heat the puree up again slowly. Season with nutmeg and leave to boil down to a creamy consistency. In the meantime, slowly roast the pumpkin seeds in a small amount of fat or dry fry in a shallow pan. (Be careful as the seeds will turn brown very quickly!) Serve the soup on warmed plates. Garnish with roasted pumpkin seeds. Drizzle over some pumpkin seed oil and stir quickly with a knife to create a decorative swirl. Serve immediately.

Pork Soup
Klachelsuppe

Serves 4–6

1 kg knuckle of pork, 1 carrot,
100 g celeriac, 1 small leek,
1 small onion, 6–8 juniper berries,
8 peppercorns, 1 bay leaf,
1 pinch of marjoram,
120 g sour cream, 1 tbsp plain flour,
1 dash of vinegar, salt, freshly milled pepper

Wash the knuckle of pork under running water and bring it to the boil in a pan containing 1 1/2 litres of water. Peel or clean the vegetables and add the juniper berries, peppercorns, and marjoram. Cook until the meat starts to loosen from the bone (approx. 1 hour). Cut the meat into bite-size pieces and place to one side. Strain the soup and bring to the boil again. Mix the sour cream and flour together until smooth and whisk into the soup. Boil the soup until it starts to thicken and season with vinegar, salt and freshly milled pepper. Add the meat to the soup and reheat.

In Styria, this soup is often served with Buckwheat Mash (for recipe see p. 33).

Knuckle Aspic with Kernel Oil
Haxlsulz mit Kernöl

Serves 4–6

1 1/2 kg knuckle of pork,
1 kg soup bones (from calf and beef),
1 large carrot, 200 g celeriac, 1 large leek,
2 onions, 1 tbsp butter, 100 ml white wine,
salt, grated zest of 1 unwaxed lemon,
1 tbsp of finely chopped parsley,
2 hard-boiled eggs, 2 red onions cut into rings,
1 tbsp cider vinegar, 2 tbsp pumpkin seed oil,
freshly milled black pepper

Wash the knuckle and the soup bones well. Peel or clean the vegetables. Cover the knuckle and the diced vegetables with water and cook until the meat is soft

(approx. 1 1/2 hours). Strain (leave stock to one side) and leave the knuckle to cool under cold running water. Remove the meat from the bone and dice it as well as the vegetables. Peel the onions and chop finely.
Heat the butter in a pan, sweat the onions, add the wine, diced vegetables and meat. Bring everything to the boil until the liquid has almost completely evaporated. Season with salt, lemon zest and parsley. Pour over the stock (previously placed aside). Arrange the shelled and sliced eggs in an appropriately sized bowl. Pour the jellied liquid into the bowl and leave to cool. Just before serving, place the bowl in hot water and tip it upside down to turn out the aspic. Cut into slices, garnish with red onion rings, cider vinegar and pumpkin seed oil and season with salt and pepper.

To ensure that the aspic will set sufficiently, you may add another 1–2 soaked gelatine sheets to the hot liquid.

Carp in Herbs and Aspic
Gesulzter Wurzelkarpfen

Serves 4–6
500 g carp fillet (skin on),
salt, vinegar, 2 onions, 1 carrot,
100 g celeriac, 1 small leek,
6–8 peppercorns,
1 bay leaf, 12 gelatine sheets,
3 hard-boiled eggs,
a few leaves of curly parsley
and chervil

If necessary, bone, scale and vigorously rub salt into the flesh of the carp the previous day. Add a good dash of vinegar to some salted water and bring to the boil. Place the fillet into a bowl, pour the boiling water over it and leave it to soak away from the heat for at least 20 minutes.

In the meantime, peel the onion and chop coarsely, peel and clean the vegetables and cut into fine strips. Tie the herbs in cheesecloth or a muslin bag and simmer in ample salted water for about 30 minutes.

Remove the carp from the vinegar water, place it into the prepared herb broth and let it simmer just under boiling point for about 15 minutes. Take out the carp – remove any remaining bones if necessary – and remove the skin. (If preferred you may leave this on). Sieve the broth and boil it down on a high heat to about 1/2 litre. Then add and dissolve the soaked and pressed gelatine in the water. Allow the broth to cool slightly. Pour the cooled broth into an appropriate tray or bowl and leave it to set in the fridge. Shell the eggs, cut into slices and as soon as the aspic has set, layer the eggs in with the herbs. Cover over with some of the broth and leave it to cool down further. Then put in the pieces of carp and vegetables and baste with the remaining broth. Leave to cool for about 12 hours, or overnight. Before turning out, briefly dip the bowl in hot water. Garnish with parsley and chervil leaves and serve.

Wurzelkarpfen may also be eaten as a warm main course. To do this, the carp must be cooked as described in the herb broth and then served with vegetables sautéed in butter.

Salads & Side Dishes

Viennese Style Potato Salad
Erdäpfelsalat auf Wiener Art

750 g waxy potatoes, 1 small onion,
200 ml warm beef stock, 2 tbsp oil,
2 tbsp cider vinegar, salt, freshly milled pepper,
1 pinch of sugar, a dash of mustard,
1 tbsp chopped chives

Cook the potatoes and peel them while still hot. Leave them to steam for a moment, then cut into thin slices. Peel the onion and chop finely.

Prepare a marinade using the warm beef stock, oil, vinegar, onion, salt and pepper. Mix these together with sugar and mustard, according to taste. Pour the marinade over the potatoes. Serve the potato salad warm, garnished with chives.

According to old Viennese tradition, the potato salad was often served with lamb's lettuce or dandelion leaves.

If you cut the potatoes whilst warm into the marinade, the individual slices will not stick together.

Potato Salad with Mayonnaise
Erdäpfelsalat mit Mayonnaise

750 g long waxy potatoes,
salt, freshly milled pepper, some vinegar solution,
200 g mayonnaise (homemade if possible),
1 tbsp chopped chives

Cook the potatoes and peel them while still hot. Place in a bowl and season with salt and pepper. Pour vinegar solution over and leave to cool. Then mix half of the mayonnaise with the potatoes. Coat the potato salad with the remaining mayonnaise and refrigerate. Mix through before serving. Season the salad to taste and garnish with chives.

It is not typical, though not at all unusual, to dress the Potato Salad with finely chopped onions.

Beef Salad
Rindfleischsalat

For the salad:
500 g boiled beef, 300 g boiled waxy potatoes,
3 pickled gherkins, 3 tomatoes, 1 green pepper
For the marinade:
1 tsp mustard, 6 tbsp vegetable oil
(or pumpkin seed oil), 2 tbsp cider vinegar,
salt, freshly milled pepper,
1 tbsp finely chopped mixed herbs,
2 onions, 2 anchovy fillets
To garnish:
2 hard-boiled eggs

Clean the beef and remove any fat. Cut the meat into thin slices and slice the potatoes. Coarsely dice the pickled gherkins. Mix all these together in a large bowl. For the marinade, mix the mustard, oil, vinegar, salt, pepper and herbs thoroughly with the peeled onions and finely chopped anchovy fillets. Pour the marinade over the beef and leave this to soak through for at least 1–2 hours by stiring the mixture once in a while.
Just before serving, remove the stem ends from the tomatoes and cut into slices. Clean the peppers and cut into strips. Mix them both into the salad. Shell the hard-boiled eggs, cut into eight wedges and garnish the salad with them.

A great way to use up any left-over Tafelspitz (boiled beef) etc.

Bread Dumplings
Semmelknödel

200 ml milk, 60 g melted butter, 3 eggs,
2–3 tbsp sour cream, salt, freshly milled pepper,
1 tbsp finely chopped parsley, 320 g stale bread rolls
or breadcrumbs, 4–5 tbsp plain flour

Mix the milk with the butter, eggs, cream, salt, pepper and parsley in a bowl. Pour this over the bread or breadcrumbs into another bowl and mix well. Leave to rest for approx. 15–20 minutes. Then fold in the flour. With moistened hands, shape the dumplings (not too small) into balls and boil them in ample salted water for 15–20 minutes, until they rise to the surface. Remove from water, leave to drain and serve.

Bread dumplings are ideal to serve with the juices from meat, ragouts or sauces, e.g. mushroom sauce.

Some older recipes suggest preparing the bread dumplings with roasted onions. If you steam rather than boil the dumplings you can get away with using less flour, or even none at all. The same applies to the Alt-Wiener Serviettenknödel (Old Viennese Style Napkin Dumplings), which are oblong-shaped, wrapped in a napkin, tied up at both ends and cooked in gently simmering salted water for 40–50 minutes, before being cut into slices of a thickness of about 2 centimeters.

Waldviertler Dumplings
Waldviertler Knödel

1 kg floury potatoes, 2 tbsp semolina,
2 tbsp potato flour, salt

Boil half of the potatoes in a pan until soft and leave to cool. Peel and grate using a large grater. Peel the other half of the potatoes and grate raw into a bowl with cold water. Leave to stand for 1/2 hour, then squeeze the potatoes in a tea towel removing as much of the moisture as possible (keep the strained water to one side). Mix the raw potatoes with the boiled potatoes. Carefully pour off the strained water from the bowl. Loosen the deposited starch from the bottom of the bowl, mix with the semolina, potato flour and salt. Mix the potatoes into a smooth dough.

With slightly moistened hands, shape the dumplings (not too small) from the dough.

Bring some salted water to the boil. Place the dumplings in the water. Depending on size, leave to simmer for about 15–20 minutes. Remove from water, leave to drain and serve.

In Lower Austria and Vienna, Waldviertler Dumplings are a typical side dish to crispy roast pork and roast goose. These are often also stuffed with left-over meat, bacon or dripping and served with sauerkraut as a separate dish.

Mini Dumplings
Nockerl

500 g plain flour, 3 eggs, 2 egg yolks,
1 pinch of salt, 150 ml milk, approx. 100 ml water,
melted butter (optional)

In a bowl mix the flour with the eggs, egg yolks and salt. Mix the water and the milk together and add to the mixture to ensure that the dough is not too firm. Bring ample salted water to the boil in a large pan. Pass the dough through a Spätzlehobel (see glossary) directly into the boiling water and simmer for 2–3 minutes, until the Mini Dumplings rise to the surface. (Boil the Nockerl in smaller amounts to avoid boiling over). Take them out of the water using a slotted spoon, run under cold water and leave to drain. If desired, toss in melted butter or serve according to your preference.

Nockerl go very well with ragouts, particularly veal goulash. They can also be served au gratin or mixed with bacon and eggs as a separate dish. This classic Nockerl recipe was popular in its many different varieties in "old Austrian" cuisine. In Hungary, Nockerl are called Galuska, and the people of Vorarlberg differentiate, depending on shape, between the longer variety, Spätzle, and the shorter variety, Knöpfle.

Green Beans with Dill
Dillfisolen

750 g green beans,
1 pinch of baking soda, 1 tbsp butter,
1 tbsp plain flour, 200 ml hot beef stock, salt,
200 g sour cream, freshly milled pepper,
1 dash of white wine vinegar,
1 tbsp of finely chopped dill

Clean the beans, removing any stringy bits. Cut into bite-sized pieces and boil in salted water – in which the baking soda (to help the beans retain their colour) should already have been dissolved – until soft in the centre. Strain the beans and briefly run under cold water.

Melt the butter in a pan, stir in the flour and lightly sauté. Pour in the hot beef stock and stir with a whisk until smooth. After a few minutes, reduce the heat right down and then stir in the sour cream, followed by the beans. Season with salt, pepper and vinegar to taste. Sprinkle dill on top and serve the dish after brief reheating.

Dillfisolen is not just thought of as a classic accompaniment for Tafelspitz; it equally complements other boiled meat dishes, such as boiled beef shank, boiled beef tongue etc.

Carinthian Breaded Green Beans
Kärntner Stranggerl

1 onion, 250 g streaky bacon,
500 g green beans,
2 tbsp lard or oil,
1/4 l hot beef stock,
125 g stale white bread,
salt, freshly milled pepper,
butter flakes

Finely chop the peeled onion and the bacon. Wash the beans removing any stringy bits. Sweat the onion and bacon in a pan with the hot lard or oil until soft, but not browned. Pour the hot beef stock over and leave to cook. Add the beans. Cover and cook for about 20 minutes until al dente.

In the meantime, remove the crust from the bread and rub into fine breadcrumbs. Season the green beans with salt and pepper, combine with the breadcrumbs and mix everything well. Garnish with some butter flakes and serve hot.

Kärntner Stranggerl are a very popular side dish for roasted or braised lamb, but also make an excellent main course when served with new potatoes.

Upper Austrian Style Sauerkraut
Oberösterreichisches Sauerkraut

500 g sauerkraut,
1 bay leaf, 6 juniper berries,
6 peppercorns,
100 g streaky bacon (complete with rind),
1–2 tbsp melted butter,
approx. 1 tbsp instant flour (see glossary) for dredging,
150–200 ml hot beef stock, salt,
freshly milled pepper

Place the sauerkraut in a pan of cold water. Tie herbs in a cheesecloth or muslin bag. Cut the rind from the bacon and add this and the herbs to the sauerkraut. Bring everything to the boil and simmer for 30–45 minutes, depending on the desired texture. Drain off the water and remove the bacon rind and herbs.
Cut the bacon into small cubes. Melt the butter in a pan and sauté the bacon cubes. Sprinkle the flour over and leave it to lightly sauté. Pour the beef stock over. Gradually stir in the sauerkraut and leave everything to cook through for a few minutes. Season with salt and pepper.

In Vienna, sauerkraut is usually prepared with onions, sugar and caraway rather than bacon and the flour compound. It can also be served with tomato purée to create tomato cabbage.

Viennese Cabbage
Wiener Kohlgemüse

1 cabbage (approx. 1 kg),
salt, 100 g streaky bacon,
1 tbsp butter, 1 tbsp plain flour,
1/4 l hot beef stock,
1 clove of garlic, freshly milled pepper

Remove the outer leaves of the cabbage, cut it into halves, remove the stalk and cut the rest into thin strips – preferably using a mandoline. Cook until soft in boiling salted water for 30–45 minutes. Drain and squeze out the excess liquid. Chop the bacon very finely. Fry off in hot butter. Dredge in the flour and stir until a light roux forms. Pour the hot beef stock over and leave to cook whilst continuously stirring with a whisk until the liquid starts to turn to a creamy consistency. Add the cabbage. Season with the peeled and crushed garlic, salt and pepper. Briefly reheat and then serve.

In haute cuisine, the cabbage is mixed with more cream just before serving. An old housewife trick is to boil the cabbage with stale bread crusts or potatoes to lessen the distinctive cabbage smell. Cabbage is particularly popular as side dish to Siedefleisch (boiled beef) or burgers.

Apple-Horseradish Sauce
Apfelkren

2 tbsp freshly grated horseradish,
some hot stock, 1 tbsp sugar, salt,
1 dash of vinegar, 1 tbsp oil,
2–3 sour apples, juice of 1 lemon

Pour the hot stock over the freshly grated horseradish to remove its superficial tangy sharpness. Add sugar, salt, vinegar and oil. Peel, quarter and core the apples and grate them finely. Immediately mix in the lemon juice and stir in the horseradish.

Apple-Horseradish Sauce is an important a side dish to Viennese Siedefleisch, but it also lends very well to cold poultry dishes or cold sliced meats.

Snacks & Small Meals

Innviertl Style Bacon Dumplings
Innviertler Speckknödel

Serves 4–6
500 g floury potatoes,
salt, 1 egg, approx. 300 g flour
(preferably half instant –
see glossary –, half plain),
salt, flour for dusting the surface,
300 g bacon

Peel potatoes and boil in salted water. Drain and leave to steam for a while. Whilst still hot grate (using a grater) or mash (with a ricer). Form a potato dough by kneading together with the egg, flour and a little salt. Shape the dough into a roll, and cut into 12 even-sized pieces. Roll these on a floured surface, forming equal-sized dough circles. Chop the bacon finely and place some of the chopped pieces onto each dough circle. Roll these into small dumplings and press down well. Boil up an ample amount of salted water in a pan and gently simmer the dumplings until they rise to the surface.

These classic dumplings, which are particularly popular in Upper Austria, can also be stuffed with dripping or a meat/sausage mixture seasoned with garlic, parsley, salt, pepper and butter. As is tradition, these can then be served with sauerkraut.

Egg Dumplings
Eiernockerl

For the dough:
salt, 300 g plain flour, 2 eggs, 2 egg yolks,
2 tbsp melted butter, 125 ml milk
For the egg mixture:
3 tbsp clarified butter or butter,
8 eggs, 2 tbsp sour cream, salt,
freshly milled pepper
To garnish:
chopped chives

In a large, wide pan, bring an ample amount of salted water to the boil. In a bowl quickly form a smooth dough (not too stiff) from the flour, eggs, egg yolks, melted butter, milk and salt and immediately press it through a Spätzlehobel (see glossary) or coarse grater directly into simmering water. Stir, simmer for a little while longer, drain off the Nockerl and run under cold water.
For the egg mixture, heat the clarified butter or normal butter in a large pan and toss the well drained Nockerl in it. Mix the eggs, cream, salt and pepper together and pour it over the Nockerl. Leave to lightly sauté (the eggs should still be creamy). Stir well and season with salt and pepper to taste. Garnish with chives. Serve with a green salad.

Buckwheat Mash
Steirischer Heidensterz

1 tbsp salt,
approx. 330 g buckwheat flour,
3 tbsp hot lard or oil,
100 g smoked bacon

Bring 1 litre of salted water to the boil. Gradually but quickly add the buckwheat flour, but do not stir in. With the handle of a wooden spoon create a hole in the middle of the mixture and leave it to simmer on a low heat for 20 minutes. If neccessary re-form the hole. At the end of the simmering time, slowly drain off the water. Loosen the mixture using a fork and pour the hot lard or oil over it. Leave to stand a while and in the meantime dice the smoked bacon finely and fry until crisp. Pour the crispy bacon bits over the mixture and serve with green salad, if desired.

Heidensterz, also known as Hadnsterz, allegedly owes its name to the pagan cavaliers, who brought it over to Austria from the East. Heidensterz is generally served as a side dish. In many rural households in Styria – as well as in Carinthia – it is served for breakfast with Häferlkaffee (see glossary). It is regarded as an essential side dish to pork soup (for recipe see p. 13).

Cabbage and Pasta Bake
Krautfleckerl

1 cabbage, salt, 1 large onion,
150 g clarified butter or butter, 1 tbsp sugar,
freshly milled pepper, approx. 250 ml hot beef stock,
250 g Fleckerl (see glossary)

Remove the outer leaves of the cabbage, cut it into halves, remove the stalk and cut the rest into thin strips – preferably using a mandoline. Put the cabbage into a bowl, season well with salt and leave to stand with a lid on until it becomes moist. Drain off the excess liquid. In the meantime, peel and finely chop the onion.
Heat the clarified butter or butter in a casserole. Sprinkle the sugar into it and caramelise. Add the onion and sweat off until soft. Add the cabbage, salt and pepper, pour over some beef stock and stew for 35 minutes until soft. In the meantime bring ample salted water to the boil. Cook the Fleckerl until al dente, strain and run under cold water. Drain the Fleckerl and mix in with the cabbage, stir thoroughly and leave to steam briefly. Season with salt and pepper to taste and serve with lettuce.

Ham and Pasta Bake
Überbackene Schinkenfleckerl

Serves 4–6

250 g Fleckerl (see glossary), salt, 5 tbsp butter, 2 egg yolks, 6–7 tbsp grated cheese (Gouda, Emmental cheese etc.), 3 tbsp sour cream, freshly milled pepper, 1 pinch of freshly ground nutmeg, 250 g ham or boiled smoked meat, 2 egg whites, butter and breadcrumbs to line baking dish, 1–2 tbsp breadcrumbs to coat, some butter flakes to glaze

Cook the Fleckerl in ample salted water until al dente, strain and run under cold water. Leave to drain well. Cream butter until fluffy. Mix with the egg yolks, half of the grated cheese and the cream. Season with salt, pepper and nutmeg. Dice the ham or smoked meat finely. Mix into the butter mixture with the Fleckerl.
Preheat the oven to 190 °C. Beat the egg whites with some salt until stiff and fold into the mixture. Grease a casserole with butter and coat with breadcrumbs.
Fill the baking dish with the Fleckerl mix. Sprinkle on the remaining cheese and breadcrumbs, and place butter flakes on top. Bake in the preheated oven for 40–45 minutes until golden. Cut out even-sized pieces and serve with a leafy green salad.

For a simplified version, just mix the Fleckerl with the ham and toss in plenty of clarified butter or butter.

Stuffed Cheesy Dough Pockets
Kärntner Kasnudeln

Serves 8

For the dough:

250 g plain flour, 1 egg, 180 ml water or milk, 1 pinch of salt

For the filling:

300 g boiled potatoes, 1 onion, 3–4 tbsp butter, 4–5 tbsp mixed herbs (mint, chervil, parsley, chives), 700 g low-fat, "dry" Quark (see glossary, preferably grainy curd or cottage cheese), 1 egg yolk, 125 g sour cream, salt

Extras:

flour for the worktop, clarified butter or dripping for basting

For the dough, knead together the flour, egg, water or milk, and salt on a floured work surface. Wrap the smooth dough in clingfilm and leave to rest in a cool place for 1 hour.

In the meantime, prepare the filling. Pass the cooked and peeled potatoes through a sieve. Peel and finely

chop the onion. Heat the butter. Add the herbs and the onion to the butter and leave to soften for a short time, then leave to cool. Mix the sieved Quark with the herbs, potatoes, onion, egg yolks, cream and salt. Shape small balls from the mixture.
Roll out the dough to about 3 millimetres, cut into square pieces of about 8–10 centimetres and place a ball of Quark on top of each piece. Fold the dough over itself to form a pocket, leaving a good centimetre edge around the filling. Seal well and cut out crescent shapes of equal sizes using a pastry wheel. If your talents allow, give the dough pockets a crinkly decorative edge using your thumb and forefinger (see tip below).
Bring an ample amount of salted water to the boil. Place the dough pockets into the pan and simmer on a low heat for approx. 10 minutes, stirring occasionally. Remove and drizzle with the butter or dripping. Serve with a leafy green salad or tomato salad.

This heartier Carinthian version of the Italian ravioli is often stuffed with meat, dripping, sauerkraut or prunes.

In Carinthia, it is particularly important that a cook is able to produce a decorative, scalloped edge. This is much easier to do if egg is omitted from the dough mixture. According to an old proverb heard between the Gail and Drau rivers in Carinthia: "A maid, that is not able to scallop, gets no husband."

Stuffed Peppers in Tomato Sauce
Gefüllte Paprika in Paradeisersauce

For the stuffed peppers:
4 large peppers, salt, 1 onion,
1 tbsp chopped parsley,
1 tbsp clarified butter,
500 g mixed minced meat (beef, pork, veal),
150 g pre-cooked rice,
1 egg, 1–2 cloves of garlic,
freshly milled pepper,
1 pinch of marjoram

For the tomato sauce:
2 small onions, 600 g tomatoes,
2 tbsp butter or oil, 2 tbsp plain flour,
250 ml hot beef stock,
salt, freshly milled pepper,
1 pinch of sugar,
1 dash of vinegar

Extras:
butter to drizzle,
clarified butter to sauté

For the stuffed peppers, cut the top off the peppers, remove the stalk and place to one side. Wash the peppers and blanch in boiling salted water. After 5 minutes, drain off the water and run the peppers under cold water. With the opening pointing downwards, leave to drain on a piece of kitchen paper. In the meantime, peel and chop the onion, and lightly sauté in the clarified butter together with the parsley and then leave to cool.

Preheat the oven to 180 °C. Knead the minced meat together with the cooked rice, egg, sautéed onion, parsley, peeled and crushed garlic, salt, pepper, marjoram and some water to form a smooth dough. Fill the peppers with the mixture and close with the appropriate lid. Put in a baking dish, drizzle with ample melted butter and roast in the oven for 30 minutes.

In the meantime, prepare the tomato sauce. Peel and chop the onions finely. Remove the stalks from the tomatoes and roughly chop.

Heat the fat in a casserole and lightly sauté the onions. Sprinkle in the flour and stir it in. Pour the hot stock over. Add the chopped tomatoes. Season with salt, pepper, sugar and vinegar and cook for 30 minutes.

Remove the baking dish from the oven. Pour the tomato sauce over the stuffed peppers and leave to bake in the oven for a further 20 minutes. Serve with traditional boiled potatoes.

Main Dishes

Fish Dishes

Carp in Beer Batter
Karpfen in Bierteig

4 large or 8 small carp fillets (approx. 800 g in total), salt, juice of 1/2 lemon, some flour to coat the fillets

For the beer batter:

2 eggs, 150 g plain flour, approx. 200 ml beer, 2 tbsp melted butter or vegetable oil, salt

Extras:

clarified butter for frying, lemon slices to garnish

For the beer batter: Separate the eggs. Stir the flour with the yolks, beer, melted butter or oil, and a pinch of salt to form a smooth mixture. Leave to rest for 30 minutes.

In the meantime, wash the carp fillets, pat dry, skin and bone. Season with plenty of salt on both sides, drizzle with some lemon juice and roll in flour. Beat the egg whites until stiff and fold into the beer batter.

In a large pan, heat up a generous amount of clarified butter. Dip the carp fillets into the beer batter and fry both sides in the hot fat until golden-brown. Remove the fillets and leave to drain of excess fat on a piece of kitchen paper. Serve garnished with a slice of lemon. Parsley potatoes and lamb's lettuce complement this dish well.

For parsley potatoes toss little cooked potatoes in heated butter and sprinkle generously with freshly chopped parsley.

Trout à la Philippine Welser
Bachforelle Philippine Welser

4 ready-to-cook brook trout, salt,
some milk and flour to coat the fish

For the mayonnaise:

2 egg yolks, some mustard,
1 dash of lemon juice, salt, freshly milled pepper,
approx. 250 ml oil, 1 pinch of sugar,
1 pinch of anchovy paste,
1 tsp tomato purée, freshly grated horseradish

Extras:

vegetable oil for frying, lemon slices to garnish

For the mayonnaise whisk the egg yolks together with the mustard, lemon juice, salt and pepper until smooth. Add the oil drop by drop at first, stirring continuously, and then add in a slow trickle until the mayonnaise starts to thicken. Finish off by seasoning to taste with anchovy paste, tomato purée and grated horseradish. Wash the trout thoroughly inside and out, and pat dry. Salt both the inside and outside well. Put some milk in a soup bowl and flour onto a flat plate. First, dip the fish in the milk and then roll in the flour.
Heat the oil in a pan and fry the fish on both sides (15 minutes in total) until golden. Remove the fish and dab with some kitchen paper or let the fat drip away. Garnish with some slices of lemon and serve with the prepared mayonnaise. A fresh leafy green salad with crispy diced bacon and new potatoes serve as a great side dish.

This recipe is named after Philippine Welser, who in 1557 married Archduke Ferdinand II of the Habsburg dynasty in secret. The marriage was later made official. Philippine wrote Austria's first cookbook, which today is kept in the Austrian National Library.

Sheat Fish in Apple-Horseradish Sauce
Waller mit Apfelkren überbacken

750 g sheat fish fillets, juice of 1 lemon, salt,
1 small onion, 2 tbsp butter, 3 apples,
30 g freshly grated horseradish,
butter for the baking dish, 1 egg, 250 g sour cream

Preheat the oven to 180 °C. Wash the fish fillets and pat dry. Cut into thick strips. Marinate with half of the lemon juice and season with salt. Peel and finely chop the onion. Sweat the onion in the butter. Add the sheat fish and sauté lightly all around. Peel, quarter, core and grate the apples. Drizzle over the rest of the lemon juice and mix with the horseradish. Lay out the sautéed fish pieces next to each other in a buttered baking dish and coat in the apple-horseradish sauce. Cover and place into the preheated oven for approx. 20 minutes. Remove the lid. Mix the egg and cream together and pour over the fish. Bake for a further 5–8 minutes. Dill potatoes are the perfect companion for this dish.

For dill potatoes toss cooked potatoes in heated butter and sprinkle generously with freshly chopped dill.

Meat Dishes

Wiener Schnitzel

4 veal cutlets
(boneless chops from leg or loin, each 180 g),
salt, 150 g flour (preferably half instant –
see glossary –, half plain), 1 dash of lemon juice,
2 eggs, 150 g breadcrumbs,
clarified butter or oil for sautéing,
1–2 tbsp butter, 1 lemon slice to garnish

Beat the cutlets well with a meat mallet (preferably under some clingfilm), pierce the meat several times with a skewer so that the breadcrumb coating will stick better later. Season with salt all over. Prepare the breadcrumb coating on 3 soup plates: In one dish place some sieved flour, in another the lemon juice mixed with the beaten eggs, finally put the breadcrumbs in the last dish. Roll the cutlets in the flour, coating them all over, then dip them in the egg and leave them to drip briefly. Then roll in the breadcrumbs and, using the back of a fork, gently press on the breadcrumb coating; this will cause a bubble to form when frying.

Heat plenty of fat in a pan. Place the cutlets in the pan and sauté each side for about 2–3 minutes until golden. Whilst doing so, repeatedly rock the pan gently from side to side so that the hot fat "washes around" the cutlets. About 1 minute before cooking is complete, add some butter to give the cutlets an even more refined "nutty" aroma. Remove the schnitzel from the pan with a spatula and leave to drip on a piece of kitchen paper. Serve with parsley potatoes (for recipe see tip p. 41) and slices of lemon (the juice of the lemon should be gently drizzled over the schnitzel).

Real Wiener Schnitzel can only be made from veal (otherwise they must be referred to as Schweineschnitzel – pork schnitzel). They must not be cooked in a deep fryer and must preferably be fried in clarified butter.

A popular variation is the schnitzel "Cordon Bleu" which is filled with ham and Emmental cheese and then finished off in the same way as a traditional Wiener Schnitzel.

The Wiener Schnitzel originates from the south of Vienna. Field Marshall Radetzky learned of this dish whilst in Milan (however, the Milanese make it with veal chops, olive oil and no flour) and introduced it – according to historical documents – to the Vienna Royal Court. However, breaded meat has been a speciality of Eastern European cuisine for a long time.

Butter Schnitzel
Butterschnitzel

2 stale bread rolls, milk for soaking,
600–700 g minced shoulder of veal, breadcrumbs (optional), 2 eggs, salt, freshly milled pepper, 4 tbsp clarified butter, approx. 200 ml hot beef stock, butter flakes, 1 tsp flour and 2 tbsp sour cream for thickening (optional)

Soak the breadcrumbs in milk, squeeze out the excess milk. Add the minced meat and eggs and mix into a fluffy, light dough. Season with salt and pepper and, using wet hands, form rissoles from the mixture. If desired, roll in breadcrumbs.
Preheat the oven to 180 °C. Heat the clarified butter in a large pan and fry off the rissoles on both sides until golden brown. Remove from the pan and place next to each other in a flame-proof baking dish. Pour the beef stock into the pan to deglaze it, scraping any residue from the base. Reduce down to two thirds on a high heat. Pour this gravy over the rissoles. Sprinkle a few butter flakes on top and bake for a further 20 minutes in the pre-heated oven. Remove from it. If required, sprinkle flour into the sauce and thicken with some sour cream. Serve the Butter Schnitzel on warmed plates, cover with the reduced sauce and serve with mashed potatoes.

To give the schnitzel a more succulent flavour, finely chop the meat with a sharp knife rather than mincing it through a grinder.

Tyrol Style Liver
Tiroler Leber

600–700 g calf's liver,
salt, freshly milled pepper,
flour for rolling and dredging,
1 onion, 2–3 tbsp clarified butter or oil,
3 tbsp butter, approx. 150 ml beef stock,
1–2 tsp capers, grated zest of 1 unwaxed lemon,
lemon juice, 3–4 tbsp cream,
fried bacon strips to garnish (optional)

Remove the skin from the calf's liver, taking out any sinews, and cut into strips. Season both sides with salt and pepper and dredge one side with flour. Peel and finely chop the onion.

Heat the clarified butter in a pan. Then, on a high heat, quickly fry off the liver first on the floured side and after that all around. Remove from the pan and keep in a warm place.

Pour off the excess fat and briefly heat up the butter. Lightly sweat the onion in the butter, dredge in 1 tablespoon of flour and deglaze with the beef stock.

In the meantime, finely chop the capers and stir into the sauce along with the grated lemon zest. Stir briefly and then add the whisked cream. Leave to boil vigorously for a few minutes. Season to taste with some lemon juice. Place the liver strips back in the pan and leave to briefly heat up again but not cook. If desired, garnish with strips of fried bacon and serve with roast potatoes and a green leafy salad.

Viennese Style Veal Offal
Wiener Salonbeuschel

approx. 600 g calf's lung,
1 carrot, 1 small leek, 100 g celeriac,
2 small onions, 1 calf's heart,
6 peppercorns, 3 allspice berries,
1 bay leaf, 1 sprig of thyme, salt,
40 g clarified butter, 30 g plain flour,
1 tsp capers, 1 finely chopped anchovy,
1 peeled garlic clove,
grated zest of 1 unwaxed lemon,
1 tbsp finely chopped parsley,
freshly milled pepper,
1 pinch of sugar, 1 dash of vinegar,
1 pinch of ground marjoram,
1 pinch of mustard,
2 tbsp sour cream,
2 tbsp whipped cream,
1 dash of lemon juice,
4 tbsp goulash gravy to dress (optional)

Remove the windpipe and gullet from the calf's lung, rinse well and pierce on all sides several times with a sharp pointed knife; this will enable the cooking water to seep into the lungs. Peel the vegetables, clean and chop them into small pieces. Halve 1 onion, unpeeled, and fry off in a fat-free pan (cut side down) until dark brown. Peel the other onion and dice finely. Place the lungs and the cleaned heart in cold water, bring to the boil and cook until soft along with the vegetables, fried

onion, season with thyme and salt. Take out the lungs after about 1 hour and leave to cool in cold water. Boil the heart in the mixture for at least another 30 minutes; it should be soft after this time. Remove the heart and place the stock to the side. Cut the heart and lungs into very fine strips.
Heat the clarified butter, sauté the flour in it until light brown. Flavour with the finely chopped capers, diced onion, anchovy, crushed garlic, lemon zest and parsley. Leave to simmer on a low heat for a few minutes. Pour over the strained stock, stir well with a whisk and leave to simmer for 15–20 minutes until creamy. Add the cut heart and lungs and season with salt, pepper, sugar, vinegar, marjoram and mustard. As soon as the sauce has become creamy, fold in the sour cream and the whipped cream. Leave to simmer for a further 5–10 minutes. Season to taste with some lemon juice. If desired, drizzle some hot goulash sauce over it. An ideal side dish would be Bread Dumplings (for recipe see p. 22) or fresh crusty bread rolls.

To contemporary cuisine, this classic Viennese dish has been given a modern twist. Instead of thickening with flour, puréed vegetables or crème fraîche are used. This is often served with al dente julienne vegetables.

Tafelspitz with Traditional Trimmings
Tafelspitz mit klassischen Beilagen

For the Tafelspitz (see glossary):
500 g beef bones, 1 kg Tafelspitz,
salt, 1 onion, 1 carrot, 1 small leek,
100 g celeriac, 2 tomatoes (optional),
2 peeled, crushed garlic cloves,
1 bay leaf, 6 peppercorns,
2 tbsp chopped chives, coarse salt,
4 slices of toasted brown bread (optional),
4 boiled slices of marrow
(from the marrowbone)
For the chive sauce:
1 garlic clove, 1/2 white roll (no crust),
milk for soaking, 4 soft-boiled egg yolks,
250 ml oil, 1 dash of white wine vinegar
or cider vinegar, salt,
freshly milled white pepper,
1 pinch of sugar, 3 tbsp sour cream,
4 tbsp chopped chives

Wash the bones well and place into plenty of boiling salted water along with the Tafelspitz. Halve the onion and fry off in a fat-free pan (cut side down) until quite dark. After 45 minutes, add the fried onion, the washed and peeled vegetables, tomatoes (if applicable), garlic, bay leaf and pepper to the meat and cook everything for a further 1–1 1/2 hours on a medium heat; the meat should be soft after this time. In the meantime, prepare the chive sauce. Rub a bowl with crushed garlic.

Soak the white roll in milk, squeeze out the excess milk and push the rolls along with the egg yolks through a sieve directly into the bowl. Gradually add the oil and stir it in until the mixture becomes creamy. Season with vinegar, salt, pepper and sugar. Fold in the cream. Mix the chives into the sauce.
Remove the soft-boiled meat from the pan. Slice across the grain and keep warm. Before serving, sprinkle on some chives and coarse salt. Toast the brown bread, cover with the cooked slices of marrow and serve with the Tafelspitz. As well as chive sauce, complementary side dishes include: Green Beans with Dill (for recipe see p. 25) and/or Viennese Cabbage (for recipe see p. 28), Apple-Horseradish Sauce (for recipe see p. 29) and roast potatoes.

The meat adopts a greater flavour when cooked with a whole cut of Tafelspitz (approx. 2–3 kg) rather than just a piece.

Roast with Onions
Zwiebelrostbraten

4 slices of boneless prime rip or roast beef
(each approx. 200 g, tender and hung, if possible),
salt, freshly milled pepper, flour for coating the beef,
2 tbsp clarified butter, 250 g onions, sufficient oil
for sautéing, some beef stock to marinade,
2–3 cold butter flakes

Gently tenderise the slices of meat or knead them with your fingers. Cut into the edge several times to stop the meat from curling later on. Sprinkle on salt and pepper and dredge one side with some flour.
Heat the clarified butter in a pan. Fry the meat in it, floured side down first. Fry each side for 2–3 minutes until crispy.
In the meantime, peel the onions and cut into segments. Fry in the hot oil until golden brown and leave the excess oil to drip off. Arrange the slices of meat on plates and cover with the onions. Deglaze the pan of the meat residue, leave to boil. Bind with a few flakes of cold butter and pour over the meat. Serve with roast potatoes, salted gherkins and hot mustard.

Using garlic instead of onions (in reduced quantities of course), makes a "Vanillirostbraten". The only link to the name of the dish and the vanilla spice is the fact that, in old Vienna, garlic was considered to be the "poor man's vanilla".

Beef Roulades
Rinderrouladen

4 slices boneless prime rip, roast beef or boneless beef cutlets (each 200 g), salt, freshly milled pepper, 1 tsp mustard, 1 tsp anchovy paste, 100 g streaky bacon, 1 large white onion, 1 tbsp finely chopped spiced gherkins, 1 tsp finely chopped capers, 2 tbsp breadcrumbs, 1 tbsp finely chopped parsley, 2 tbsp vegetable oil, beef stock to marinade, 1 tsp plain flour, 2 tbsp sour cream

Beat the slices of beef until thin. Season with salt and pepper and lay out flat. Coat in mustard and anchovy paste. Finely chop the bacon. Peel and finely chop the onion.

Let the fat from the bacon melt slowly in a pan and sauté the onion, gherkins, capers, breadcrumbs and parsley in it on a low heat. Spread this mixture evenly on the slices of meat and roll these into roulades. Tie with kitchen string.

Heat some oil in a casserole, fry off the roulades all around. Pour over some stock and then cover. Stew the meat slowly on a low heat for approx. 1 1/2 hours, until soft. If required, pour more stock over. Remove the cooked roulades and keep warm. Dredge flour into the sour cream and whisk. Add to the sauce to thicken it. Cut through the roulades at an angle, pour over the sauce and, if desired, serve with rice or fusilli.

Viennese Goulash
Wiener Saftgulasch

800 g streaky beef
(preferably lower leg or shoulder),
400 g onions, 4 tbsp clarified butter,
3 tbsp mild paprika,
1–2 garlic cloves, salt

Remove any large sinews or fatty bits from the beef and roughly dice. Peel the onions and slice into rings.
Heat the clarified butter in a large pan and sauté the onions on a medium heat for 20–30 minutes, stirring continuously, until golden.
Remove the pan briefly from the heat. Stir in the paprika and deglaze immediately with a little water (paprika will taste too bitter if cooked on too high a heat). Place the pan back on the cooker and add the meat. Crush and add the peeled garlic, and salt. Cover the pan with a lid, leaving it slightly ajar. Depending on the quality of meat, leave to stew for 1 1/2–2 hours, until soft. Add just enough water to barely cover the meat. Do not allow it to "drown". Again season to taste and serve with boiled potatoes.

This old Viennese Goulash is the basis of numerous further goulash variations, ranging from: Goulash Soup (liquid, hot and with diced potatoes), Potato Goulash (bacon or diced potatoes instead of meat), Fiakergulasch (beef goulash with sausages, fried eggs and pickled gherkins) through to Salongulasch (with beef fillet and potatoes) or Kalbsgulasch (with soft braised veal, a light sauce made from flour and cream for thickening and Nockerl as side dish).

Styrian Pork with Vegetables and Horseradish Sauce Krenfleisch

125 ml vinegar, 2 bay leaves,
4 peppercorns, salt,
800 g shoulder of pork,
6 carrots, 1/2 celeriac, 1 parsley root,
1/2 leek, 1 medium onion,
150 g freshly grated horseradish

Place some cold water in a pan with the vinegar, herbs and salt. Add the meat and boil for 40–45 minutes. In the meantime, peel and wash the carrots, celeriac and parsley root. Cut into thin strips. Peel the onion, wash the leek and slice both. At the end of the cooking time, add the onion, leek and root vegetables to the pan. Cook for a further 20 minutes. Remove the soft boiled meat and slice across the grain. Arrange onto a warmed plate, pour some stock over, cover with the vegetables and garnish with grated horseradish. Serve with boiled potatoes.

The horseradish sauce is often blended with dry white wine to enhance its flavour.

Roast Pork
Schweinebraten

1 kg pork with rind
(piglet, neck of pork, loin etc.),
salt, 3–4 peeled and crushed garlic cloves,
caraway seeds to garnish, some pork bones,
1/2 tbsp plain flour,
beef stock or water to baste

Pour water into a roasting pan to a depth of 2 centimeters. Bring to the boil. Place the pork in the pan with the rind facing down, bring to the boil again. Reduce the heat and leave to simmer for 10–15 minutes.
Preheat the oven to 220 °C. Take out the pork and cut into the rind at frequent intervals with a sharp knife, along the length and width of the joint. Be careful not to cut into the meat itself, otherwise it will dry out when cooking. Rub well all over with salt and garlic, sprinkle with caraway seeds. Place the washed bones into a fireproof roasting pan, as well as the roast pork (rind face up) and roast in the preheated oven for 10–15 minutes at 220 °C, then at 180–170 °C (total cooking time of 1 1/2–2 hours).
In the meantime, baste the joint in its own juices, occasionally pouring stock or water under the roast, never directly over it. Approx. 40–50 minutes before the end of the cooking time, season the rind with plenty of salt – do not baste again. As soon as the joint has roasted through, i.e. when the juices run clear when pricking with a fork, remove and leave to rest in a warm place.

In the meantime, drain off the excess meat residue. Dredge some flour onto the bones. Quickly fry off on a high heat and boil up in some water. Cook the gravy for as long as it takes to reach the desired consistency, then strain. Slice up the pork and serve the sauce in a gravy boat. Bread Dumplings (for recipe see p. 22) and Sauerkraut (for recipe see p. 27) complement this dish well.

For an authentic Bauernschmaus (Farmer's Stew), in addition to cabbage and dumplings, the Roast Pork is served with a piece of boiled smoked meat and Frankfurter sausages.

Styrian Roast Chicken
Steirisches Backhuhn

2 small ready-to-cook chickens
of 800–1000 g each (with liver),
salt, some plain flour, 2–3 eggs,
breadcrumbs to coat, vegetable oil
and 50 g clarified butter to sauté,
curly parsley and 1 lemon in slices
to garnish

Quarter the chicken into legs and breast (with wings) parts, wash, towel dry and season all over with plenty of salt. Prepare some flour, whisked egg and breadcrumbs on three separate plates. Roll all the chicken pieces, including the neck and the giblets, one after the other in the flour, then in the egg and finally in the breadcrumbs. Gently press the breadcrumb coating down all around, using the back of a fork.

Heat plenty of oil and clarified butter in a large pan. Once the fat is really hot, place the chicken pieces into it. Fry them all over for approx. 15–20 minutes until golden brown and crispy. Regulate the heat to avoid the chicken turning too brown and the bread coating crumbling off. The roast chicken is done, once the juices run clear when pricking the pieces at the joint. Only add the chicken liver about 4–5 minutes before the end of the cooking time, otherwise it will dry out. Remove the chicken from the fat and leave it to thoroughly drip dry of any excess on some kitchen paper. Then arrange on a plate. Serve garnished with a Viennese Style Potato Salad (for recipe see p. 19), curly parsley – fried off in the remaining fat – and slices of lemon.

In contrast to Styrian Roast Chicken, a Wiener Backhendl (Viennese Roast Chicken) is not roasted together with the neck, backbone and giblets (they are used for chicken soup). In upmarket eateries, the roast chicken is sometimes first boned, skinned and then coated in breadcrumbs. But unfortunately, in modern gastronomy, it is becoming more and more common to refer to breaded chicken breast as Backhuhn (roast chicken).

Desserts

Salzburg Egg Soufflé
Salzburger Nockerl

125 ml milk, 1 tbsp butter, 1 pkt. vanilla sugar, 6 egg whites, 1 pinch of salt, 3 tbsp sugar, 3 egg yolks, grated zest of 1 unwaxed lemon, 2 tbsp plain flour, butter (room temp.) for greasing the baking dish, icing sugar for decoration

In a small pan, mix the milk, butter and half of the vanilla sugar and slowly warm on a low heat. In the meantime, beat the egg whites with the salt until they form soft peaks, beat in the sugar and whisk briskly. Stir in the egg yolks with the lemon zest and the remaining vanilla sugar and gently fold into the egg whites, alternating with sieved flour.

Preheat the oven to 200 °C. Grease a suitable oval, shallow baking dish with a generous amount of butter. Just cover the base of the dish with the warmed milk/butter/sugar mixture and then carefully spoon the mixture into the dish in the shape of large pyramids, using a spatula. Bake the Nockerl in the preheated oven for approx. 8–10 minutes until golden (the peaks should just be lightly browned). Remove from the oven, dust well with icing sugar and serve immediately in the dish – as the soufflé will quickly collapse.

Legend has it that the original recipe was discovered by Salome Alt (1568–1633), the long-time concubine – a modern arrangement at this time – of the Prince Archbishop W. D. von Raitenau (1559–1617).

Apple Strudel
Apfelstrudel

For the strudel pastry:
200 g instant flour (see glossary), 2 tbsp oil
(alternatively use ready-made strudel pastry)
For the filling:
1 1/2 kg apples, 1 dash of lemon juice, 2–3 tbsp rum,
2–3 tbsp raisins, 1 pinch of cinnamon, 1 pkt. vanilla
sugar, 120 g sugar, 80 g butter, 120 g breadcrumbs
Extras:
oil for greasing, flour for dredging,
approx. 100 g melted butter for greasing,
icing sugar for decoration

To make the strudel pastry, form a mound of flour on the worktop and form a well in the centre. Mix in the oil and 120 millilitres of water with a fork, and knead the ingredients to form a soft dough. Knead well until the dough starts to lift from the worktop and is smooth and glossy. Shape into a ball and place into an oil-greased bowl. Grease the dough with oil, cover over and leave to rest for at least 1/2 hour.
Roll the dough out into a rectangle, on a tea towel dusted with flour. Brush with oil. Move both hands under the dough until you reach the middle. Gently and evenly pull the dough over the backs of both hands to a size of 70 x 70 centimetres. Close any holes that may appear. The dough should be thin enough so that you can clearly see the pattern of the cloth through it. Cut off the thick edge all the way around.

To prepare the filling, peel, quarter and core the apples. Cut them into thin slices. Mix them immediately with lemon juice, rum, raisins, cinnamon, vanilla sugar and sugar. Melt the butter in a pan and sauté the breadcrumbs until golden. Leave to cool slightly and then mix with the apples.
Brush the strudel pastry with melted butter. Spread the apple filling onto the pastry and lift the pastry using the cloth over the filling, rolling into a strudel shape. Fold the ends down well and seal.
Preheat the oven to 180 °C. Line a suitable baking tray with greaseproof paper or grease with butter. Place the strudel, seam side down, in the tray and brush again all over with plenty of melted butter. Bake for 40 minutes in the preheated oven. Remove from the oven and dust with plenty of icing sugar. Serve cold or warm.

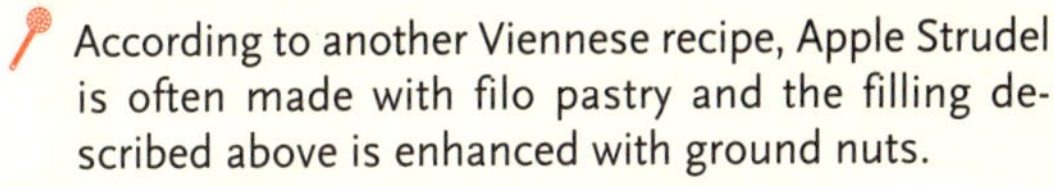

According to another Viennese recipe, Apple Strudel is often made with filo pastry and the filling described above is enhanced with ground nuts.

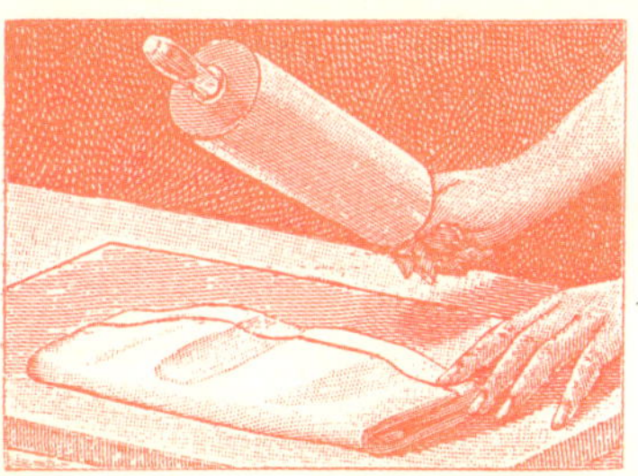

Cream Strudel with Custard
Millirahmstrudel mit Vanillesauce

Serves 6–8

1 strudel pastry recipe (see recipe p. 62, alternatively use ready-made strudel pastry or filo pastry)

For the filling:

8 stale bread rolls, 250 ml milk, 130 g butter, 110 g sugar, 4 egg yolks, 150 g sour cream, 100 g low-fat, "dry" Quark (see glossary), 1 pkt. vanilla sugar, grated zest of 1 unwaxed lemon, 4 egg whites, 60 g raisins

For the egg milk:

300–400 ml milk, 2 eggs, 2 tbsp icing sugar, 1 pkt. vanilla sugar

For the custard:

1/2 l milk, 2–3 tbsp vanilla sugar, 25 g custard powder, 100 g sugar, 2 egg yolks, 2–3 tbsp whipping cream, 1 dash of rum

Extras:

flour for the worktop, plenty of melted butter for greasing, butter for greasing the baking tray, icing sugar for decoration

Make the strudel pastry as per the recipe. To prepare the filling, remove the crusts from the bread rolls. Cut into cubes and soak in milk. Cream the butter in a bowl until fluffy. Add 100 gram sugar, egg yolks, cream, Quark, vanilla sugar and lemon zest. Stir until creamy. Squeeze out the excess milk from the bread and mix in. Beat the egg whites with the remaining sugar until stiff and fold in.

Pull the pastry on a large floured cloth as described on p. 62 and brush with melted butter. Spread the filling on about two thirds of the pastry. Sprinkle raisins over the top and gently roll up the strudel. Seal the ends well. Grease a rectangular baking tray with butter. Place the rolled strudel, seam side down, in a horseshoe shape and brush with plenty of butter. Preheat the oven to 180 °C.
For the egg milk, mix the milk, eggs, icing sugar and sugar together well. Pour about 1/4 of the mixture over the strudel and bake for 45 minutes until golden brown. During this time, keep pouring over more of the egg milk until it is all used up. In the meantime, prepare the custard. Stir about 1/3 of the milk with the vanilla sugar and the custard powder until smooth. Boil up the remaining milk with the sugar. Add the custard mixture, stirring constantly, and bring to the boil again. Remove the pan from the flame and blend in the egg yolks, whipped cream and some rum with a whisk. Remove the baked strudel from the oven, leave to cool a while and sprinkle with plenty of icing sugar. Fill small glas bowls with custard and serve warm with the strudel.

Rumour had it that the Millirahmstrudel was discovered in the 19th century in a Wienerwald inn by a cook called Milli. The fact that it was actually only a rumour has since then been proven by the existence of a 1696 handwritten Viennese "Koch-Puech" (cookbook) which contains a recipe for "Mülch Raimb Strudl zu machen". So the term "Milli" quite simply refers to the milk contained in the recipe.

Quark Dumplings with Plum Compote
Topfenknödel mit Zwetschgenröster

For the plum compote:
1 kg plums, 1 cinnamon stick, some cloves,
200 g granulated sugar, juice and grated zest
of 1 unwaxed lemon
For the dumplings:
100 g butter, grated zest of 1 unwaxed lemon,
1 pinch of salt, 4 eggs, 200 g low-fat, "dry" Quark
(see glossary), 200 g white bread (without crusts),
150 g sour cream, 120 g plain flour
Extras:
100 g butter, 80 g breadcrumbs

To make the plum compote, halve and stone the plums. Place the spices in a muslin or cloth bag, tie and boil in 150 millimetres of water with the sugar and lemon zest and juice. Add the plums and stew for approx. 20 minutes until soft. Remove the bag and leave the stewed plums in a cool place.

To prepare the dumplings, stir the butter together with the lemon zest and salt until fluffy. Mix in the eggs, strain the Quark and mix that in, too. Cut the crustless bread into small cubes and mix with the cream and flour into the dumpling mix. Leave to rest for about 20 minutes. Then form the dumplings in the size of a golf ball from the mixture.

Bring ample salted water to the boil. Place the dumplings into the water and, depending on their size, leave to simmer for 12–15 minutes until they rise to the surface. Remove from the pan and leave to drain well. Slowly melt the butter in a pan. Lightly brown the breadcrumbs on a low heat and roll the dumplings in the buttered crumbs. Serve the plum compote on the side.

Apricot Dumplings
Marillenknödel

Flour for the worktop, 250 g low-fat, "dry" Quark (see glossary), 60 g butter, 1 egg, 1 pinch of salt, 125 g plain flour, 8 stoned apricots, butter and breadcrumbs for coating, icing sugar or cinnamon sugar for decoration

On a floured worktop, knead the Quark, butter, eggs, salt and flour to form a dumpling dough. Shape into a roll and cut into 8 portions of the same size. Gently press the dough pieces together in the palms of your hand. Place the stoned apricots in the centre, pull the dough around the apricots to form round dumplings. Slowly bring to the boil a large pan of gently salted water and simmer the dumplings in it for about 10 minutes. Remove from the pan and leave to drain.
Melt plenty of butter in a pan. Lightly sauté the breadcrumbs in it. Place the dumplings into the pan and roll them in the buttered crumbs by gently rocking the pan. Serve sprinkled with icing sugar or cinnamon sugar.

This recipe can also be used to make other fruit dumplings (e.g. plums, strawberries etc.).

Dough Pockets Stuffed with Plum Jam
Powidltascherl

250 g plain flour, 2 eggs, 1 pinch of salt,
3 tbsp vegetable oil, flour for the worktop,
250 g Powidl (plum jam), 2 tbsp rum, 2 egg whites,
4 tbsp melted butter, mixture of 120 g icing sugar
and 1 pinch of cinnamon

Sieve flour onto the worktop and knead together with the eggs, salt, 3 tablespoon water and oil to form a stretchy dough. Shape into a ball and wrap in some clingfilm, and leave to rest in the fridge for about 1/2 hour.

Roll out the dough onto a floured worktop to a thickness of about 2 millimetres. Cut 8–10 centimetres squares from it. Place some of the Powidl mixed with the rum onto each square and brush the edges with egg white. Fold together into triangles. Press down the edges firmly between your fingers.

Bring a generous amount of salted water to the boil in a large pan, drop the Powidltascherl gently into the water and simmer on a low heat for about 8 minutes. Remove from the pan and leave to drain well. Roll in melted butter and serve sprinkled with a mixture of icing sugar and cinnamon.

Emperor's Pancakes
Kaiserschmarren

6 egg yolks, 50 g sugar, 250 ml milk,
200 g plain flour, 6 egg white, 1 pinch of salt,
butter for sautéing and greasing the casserole,
40 g raisins, icing sugar for decoration

Thoroughly whisk together the yolks with the sugar, milk and flour in a bowl. Beat the egg whites with the salt until stiff and gently fold into the mixture.
Melt plenty of butter in a large pan, pour in the mixture and sprinkle raisins into it. Cook for a few minutes until the underside starts to turn golden brown. Turn and, using two forks, tear the almost cooked mixture into pieces. Place the Schmarren into a greased, flameproof casserole and bake briefly in the oven preheated at 200 °C, until the mixture is just cooked, but not seared. Sprinkle with icing sugar and serve with a plum compote (for the recipe see p. 66).

According to one of many legends, the Kaiserschmarren can be traced back to a Royal Court pastry baker by the name of Leopold, who served this new creation to the Emperor Franz Joseph and Empress Elisabeth. The Empress, ever conscious of her waistline, was said to have received the calorific sweet with little enthusiasm. On the other hand, the Emperor is said to have succumbed, saying, "Ah, now let me see what 'Schmarren' (rubbish) our Leopold has cooked up again today."

Pancakes with Plum Jam
Liwanzen (Böhmische Dalken)

Liwanzen are a traditional Bohemian pastry. They can be made from a variety of dough types. This variation is made from yeast dough. Traditionally the pancakes are cooked in fat in a special pan with a shallow rounded or flat base. However, a small crêpe pan can also be used.

For the pastry:
250 ml milk, 400 g plain flour, 20 g yeast,
2 tbsp butter, 1 tbsp sugar, salt,
grated zest of 1 unwaxed lemon, 2 eggs
For the filling:
250 g Powidl (plum jam), 2 cl Slivovitz
(plum brandy), 250 g Quark (20 % fat), 2 egg yolks,
1 dash of lemon juice, 1 tbsp sugar
Extras:
flour for rolling, butter or oil for sautéing,
icing sugar or cinnamon sugar for decoration

First prepare a yeast sponge from a little milk, some flour and yeast. Cover and leave in a warm place for 1/2 hour. Mix the yeast sponge with the rest of the ingredients to form a stretchy yeast dough. Again leave this in a warm place until it doubles in volume.
For the filling, mix the Powidl with the Slivovitz. Sieve the Quark and mix in the egg yolks, lemon juice and sugar to form a cream.
Roll the dough on a floured work surface and cut out Liwanzen (round, flat pancakes) with a diameter of

8 centimetres. In a Liwanzen pan or in a suitably small crêpe pan heat the butter or oil and fry the Liwanzen on both sides until golden brown. Remove from the pan and keep in a warm place. Spread a quarter of the Liwanzen with the Powidl. On the second quarter, spread cream. Then place alternate coated and non-coated Liwanzen together and dust with icing sugar or cinnamon sugar. Plum compote provides an excellent side dish to these pancakes (for the recipe see p. 66).

Austrian Crêpes
Palatschinken

Makes 10

180 g plain flour, 3 egg yolks, 2 eggs, 1 pinch of salt, 50 g sugar, 375 ml milk, butter or vegetable oil for frying, 150 g apricot jam (room temp.), icing sugar for decoration

In a bowl, mix the flour, egg yolks, eggs, salt, sugar and milk into a smooth, thin batter. In a small pan (approx. 20 centimetres in diameter), heat a little fat and pour just enough batter into the pan to reach the side when the pan is evenly rotated. Fry until golden brown. Quickly flip over, using a spatula, taking care not to tear the Palatschinken. Fry the other side until golden brown, remove and keep warm. Cook the remaining batter in the same way. Spread each Palatschinken with apricot jam, roll them up and serve dusted with icing sugar.

Emperor's Ring Cake
Kaisergugelhupf

30 g yeast, approx. 250 ml milk, 100 g sugar,
350 g plain flour, 150 g butter, 6 egg yolks,
1 pinch of salt, 2 egg whites, butter for brushing,
flour for dredging, peeled and halved almonds
and icing sugar for decoration

Prepare a yeast sponge from the yeast, some warmed milk, a pinch of sugar and 1 tablespoon of flour. Cover and leave in a warm place. Cream some butter in a bowl, the remaining sugar, egg yolks, the remaining flour, remaining milk, salt and then mix in the risen yeast sponge. Beat the mixture briskly for as long as it takes to easily loosen from the sides of the bowl and for bubbles to start to form. Beat the egg whites until stiff and fold in.

Grease a ring cake tin with butter, dust with flour and line with almonds. Fill the baking dish with the dough. Cover and leave about 30 minutes to rise in a warm place. In the meantime preheat the oven to 170–180 °C. Bake the cake for approx. 1 hour. Leave to cool down for a short while and then turn it out. Before serving, sprinkle with icing sugar.

Sacher Torte

130 g dark chocolate,
130 g butter (room temp.),
110 g icing sugar,
6 egg yolks, 1 pkt. vanilla sugar,
6 egg whites, 110 g sugar, 130 g plain flour,
butter and flour for the cake tin,
8 tbsp apricot jam, 2 pkt. chocolate glaze

Melt the chocolate in a bain-marie. In a bowl cream the butter and icing sugar. Stir in the egg yolks and vanilla sugar. Add the melted chocolate to the mixture.
Preheat the oven to 180 °C. Beat the egg whites with the sugar until stiff and gently fold into the mixture. Finally, carefully stir in the flour. Grease a spring form cake tin well with some butter and dust with flour. Fill with the mixture and bake in the preheated oven for about 1 hour. Remove the torte, leave to cool and cut in half horizontally. Spread both halves of the torte thinly with sieved and slightly warmed jam, place the halves back together again and spread jam onto the outside, too. Melt the chocolate glaze and then coat the torte with it.

Probably the most famous Viennese torte, the Sacher Torte was "invented" by a trainee pastry chef by the name of Franz Sacher. At the time, he attended the house of the Prince Metternich as an apprentice cook and later established the Hotel Sacher, where the original recipe is kept locked away in a safe and still remains a secret today.

Linzer Torte

For the pastry:
140 g butter, 140 g sugar, 140 g ground almonds and/or hazelnuts, 140 g plain flour, 2 egg yolks (boiled and pressed through a sieve), 1 egg, 1 tsp ground coffee, 1 pinch of cinnamon, 1 pinch of clove powder, juice of 1/2 lemon

Extras:
butter for greasing the cake tin and brushing, 80 g red currant jam, 1 egg for brushing, icing sugar for decoration

Crumb together all the ingredients required to make the dough, knead quickly to form a smooth shortcrust pastry. Shape into a ball. Wrap in clingfilm and leave to rest in the fridge for 1/2 hour.

Preheat the oven to 160 °C. Split the dough. Press one half into the base of a well-greased cake tin and spread evenly with 60 gram of red currant jam. Using two thirds of the remaining dough, shape rolls with a diameter of approx. 5 millimetres and place these over the torte to form a lattice. From the remaining dough, roll out a dough rim to a thickness of about 1 centimeter and place this all the way around the edge of the torte. Press carefully but firmly. Brush the edge and the lattice with whisked egg, place the cake tin in the oven and bake until golden for approx. 45 minutes.

Leave to cool right down and spread the rest of the jam in the gaps between the lattices. Sprinkle with sieved icing sugar.

Malakoff Torte

For the torte:

180 g butter (room temp.), 200 g icing sugar, 4 egg yolks, 180 g peeled ground almonds, 150 ml whipped cream, approx. 50 sponge fingers, rum and milk for soaking

Extras:

butter for greasing the cake tin, 1/4 l whipped cream, almond slices, sponge fingers, glacé cherries for decoration

To make the torte, cream the butter in a bowl and add both the icing sugar and egg yolks. Add the almonds and whipping cream and stir until a stiff cream is formed.

Grease a spring form cake tin, briefly dip the sponge fingers one after the other in some milk mixed with rum and arrange them in the base of the tin. Line the edge with sponge fingers, which have been cut in half diagonally. Coat the sponge fingers with a generous amount of cream, lay another layer of soaked sponge fingers, and repeat this process until all the cream has been used up, with the fingers making up the last layer. Cover the torte with clingfilm and leave to cool for at least 5 hours.

Carefully release the torte from the cake tin, spread generously all over with whipped cream. Sprinkle the almond slices around the edge of the torte, cover the surface with diagonally halved sponge fingers and glacé cherries. Decorate with squirted whipped cream.

Glossary of Culinary Terms

Häferlkaffee

A large pot of coffee with hot frothy milk.

Fleckerl

Small, thin square-shaped pasta. You can use Italian tagliardi instead.

Flour

The recipes in this book use either plain flour or instant flour. By plain flour, we mean an all-purpose flour. Instant flour (see below) has been less finely milled than all-purpose flour.

Instant flour

A granular flour formulated to dissolve quickly in hot or cold liquids. It is used mainly as a thickener in sauces, gravies and other cooked mixtures. In confectionery, it is used as a replacement for flour – only available in the Alps region – which is less finely milled and therefore has better raising properties. It enhances the texture of the dough used to make strudel, Nockerl and Spätzle. Instant flour can of course be replaced with plain flour.

Quark

Often in Austrian confectionery, a very low-fat, "dry" Quark is used. To produce this type of unripened cheese, low-fat milk is replaced with rennet and/or lactobacillus bacteria, which leads to a build-up of lactic acid and the production of casein. In English-speaking countries Quark can be replaced with grainy curd or cottage cheese.

Siedefleisch

Boiled beef (see Tafelspitz).

Spätzlehobel

Spätzle press for making spätzle dumplings. There are several versions of this machine: one is similar to a vegetable grater, another is a large perforated cone with a lever that forces the dough through the holes. The third kind is like a food mill with revolving blades; this machine comes with a board (with a hole in the centre) which rests the machine on the pan.

Tafelspitz

Boiled beef. This is a typical Austrian dish. A well-hung piece of beef from the rump of a young ox is boiled together with root vegetables. Tafelspitz is the name of the cut of meat used. Austrian butchers give almost every muscle a name. The hinder beef leg alone is parted into 16 cuts: there is for example the Hüferscherzl, Hüferschwanzl, Nuss, Wadlstutzen, Gschnatter, Schwarzes Scherzl, Weißes Scherzl, Dünnes Kuegerl, Schalblattel also called Fledermaus...
So Tafelspitz is only one cut of meat which you can use for boiled beef but a very delicious one. It is located at the top of the hind leg. Alternatively, a similar cut of beef from a young ox could be used. It must be properly hung, with firm white fat (not yellow). The fat can be left on to prevent the meat from becoming dry.

Recipe Index

Soups & Starters

Salads & Side Dishes

Snacks & Small Meals

Fish Dishes

Meat Dishes

Desserts